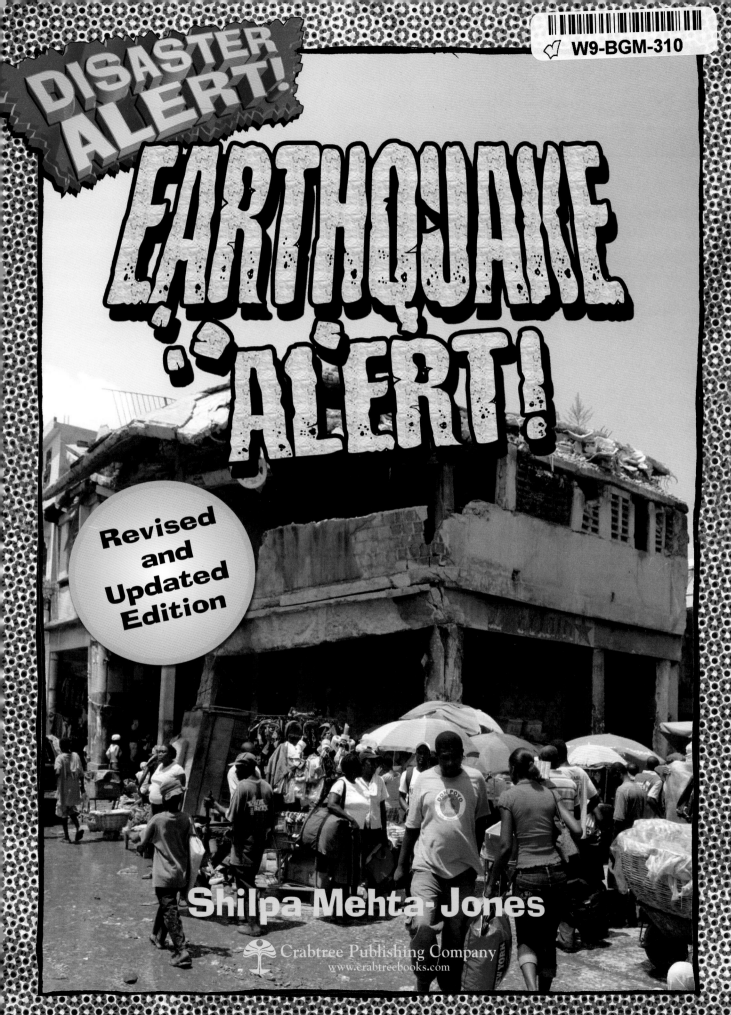

DISASTER ALERT!

EARTHQUAKE ALERT!

Revised and Updated Edition

Shilpa Mehta-Jones

Crabtree Publishing Company
www.crabtreebooks.com

For my father, Vinod—gone too soon to say goodbye
For my mother, Prafulla—as always, thank you

Researcher and editor: Adrianna Morganelli

Proofreader: Emily McMullen

Photo research: Crystal Sikkens

Cover design: Ken Wright

Editorial director: Kathy Middleton

Print and production coordinator: Katherine Berti

Prepress technicians: Margaret Amy Salter and Ken Wright

First edition:
    Coordinating editor: Ellen Rodger
    Project editor: Carrie Gleason
    Copy editors: Sean Charlebois and Ellen Rodger
    Proofreader: Adrianna Morganelli
    Book design and production coordinator: Rosie Gowsell
    Cover design: Rob MacGregor
    Indexer: Wendy Scavuzzo
    Photo research: Allison Napier

Consultant: Dr. Richard Cheel, Earth Sciences Department, Brock University

Photographs:
American Red Cross: IFRC / Eric Quintero: cover; Talia Frenkel: pages 4, 13 (bottom); Bonnie Gillespie: page 23 (bottom)
Associated Press: page 27 (bottom)
CORBIS/MAGMA: Ralph White: page 7 (bottom right); Wolfgang Kaehler: page 8; Lloyd Cluff: page 13 (top); Reuters New Media Inc.: page 15 (top); Roger Ressmeyer: pages 16, 27 (top); Bettmann: pages 17 (bottom), 29 (top)
FEMA: Adam Dubrowa: page 24 (top)
Rosie Gowsell: pages 25 (all), 29 (bottom)
iStockphoto: page 10
Keystone Press: © Charles Pertwee/Zumapress: page 20
Shutterstock: pages 1, 3, 5, 7 (top left and right), 9 (top), 19 (top), 22, 24 (bottom), 26, 28
Visuals Unlimited, Inc.: Science VU/NGDC: page 12; Inga Spence: page 18 (top)
Wikipedia: Leohotens: page 7 (bottom left); Ikluft: page 9 (bottom); Esteban Maldonado: page 15 (bottom); Shizhao: page 18 (bottom); Tubbi: page 19 (bottom); US Archiv ARCWEB ARC Identifier: 24395 NARA National Archives and Records Administration: page 21 (top); NGDC Natural Hazards Slides with Captions Header: page 23 (top)

Illustrations:
Jim Chernishenko: pages 11, 31(bottom)
Dan Pressman: pages 6–7, 8, 10, 11, 12, 14, 17 (top)
David Wysotski, Allure Illustrations pages 30–31

Cover: Most of Port-au-Prince, Haiti, was destroyed after a magnitude 7.3 earthquake hit on January 12, 2010. The earthquake caused severe damage to buildings and killed hundreds of thousands of people.
Title page: Buildings in Port-au-Prince, Haiti, still remain in hazardous condition months after the devastating earthquake hit.
Contents: People look at a fault in Utah, U.S.A.

Library and Archives Canada Cataloguing in Publication

Mehta-Jones, Shilpa
    Earthquake alert! / Shilpa Mehta-Jones. -- Rev. ed.

(Disaster alert!)
Includes index.
Issued also in electronic format.
ISBN 978-0-7787-1590-0 (bound).--ISBN 978-0-7787-1623-5 (pbk.)

    1. Earthquakes--Juvenile literature. I. Title. II. Series: Disaster alert!

QE521.3.M48 2011   j551.22   C2010-907576-5

Library of Congress Cataloging-in-Publication Data

Mehta-Jones, Shilpa, 1970-
    Earthquake alert! / Shilpa Mehta-Jones. -- Revised edition.
       p. cm. -- (Disaster Alert!)
    Includes index.
    ISBN 978-0-7787-1623-5 (pbk. : alk. paper) -- ISBN 978-0-7787-1590-0 (reinforced library binding : alk. paper) -- ISBN 978-1-4271-9618-7 (electronic pdf)
    1. Earthquakes--Juvenile literature. I. Title.
QE521.3.M44 2011
363.34'95--dc22

2010048138

Crabtree Publishing Company
www.crabtreebooks.com   1-800-387-7650

Printed in Canada/062014/TT20140513

Published in Canada
Crabtree Publishing
616 Welland Ave.
St. Catharines, Ontario
L2M 5V6

Published in the United States
Crabtree Publishing
PMB 59051
350 Fifth Avenue, 59th Floor
New York, New York 10118

Published in the United Kingdom
Crabtree Publishing
Maritime House
Basin Road North, Hove
BN41 1WR

Published in Australia
Crabtree Publishing
3 Charles Street
Coburg North
VIC, 3058

Table of Contents

Great Shakes

Earthquakes are sudden shakings of the Earth caused by massive rocks, called plates, moving under the Earth's surface. As the plates bump and grind into each other, the pressure builds as they attempt to pass each other. Over time, the strain becomes too great and the plates shoot past one another, breaking off pieces as they do. Above the Earth's surface, the land shakes and buildings crumple.

A Haitian searches through rubble for any sign of survivors, in Port-au-Prince, Haiti, after a massive earthquake hit in January 2010.

What is a disaster? A disaster is a destructive event that affects the natural world and human communities. Some disasters are predictable and others occur without warning. The ability to cope with a disaster depends on how aware and prepared a community is.

Port-au-Prince, Haiti, 2010

Explaining earthquakes

Thousands of years ago, people tried to describe what they felt, heard, and saw in ways that made sense to them. In areas of the world where earthquakes are common, people developed myths and legends to explain them. Many of these stories feature giant animals shaking Earth. Today, people understand the science behind what makes the earth quake.

Geology is an area of science that studies the origins, history, and physical structure of Earth. Geologists called seismologists study earthquakes. Seismologists monitor movements in the Earth before and after earthquakes. The information they uncover is used to design and construct new buildings that can withstand the destructive forces of earthquakes.

Quake myths

The Gabrielino native peoples of California, USA, tell a story that long ago the world was covered with water. The Great Spirit decided to make giant turtles carry the land on their backs. One day the turtles argued. Three turtles swam east, and three swam west. This caused the heavy land on their backs to shake. When they realized this, they stopped arguing. Some people say that the turtles that hold up California still argue and this makes the earth shake.

(left) A Japanese myth tells of a giant catfish that lived in mud under the earth. The catfish liked to play jokes and could only be controlled by a god named Kashima. As long as Kashima kept a mighty rock with magical powers over the catfish, the earth was still. When Kashima was not paying close attention, the catfish wriggled, causing earthquakes.

An Inside Look

The cause of earthquakes begin deep in the earth's crust, far below the surface. The Earth has four major layers. The hottest part is the core. It is solid because of all the weight pushing on it from above. The closer to Earth's surface, the cooler the planet gets.

Lithosphere

The bottom layer of the crust and the top of the mantle are called the lithosphere. The lithosphere is always slowly moving. This movement happens because the hot rock of the mantle rises up and cools as it gets closer to the crust. Once cool, the solid rock falls back down deep into the mantle. This rising and falling of the mantle rock is called a convection current.

Mantle

The mantle is outside the core. The mantle is made up of semi-solid rock, which is very hot and closely packed. The temperature of the mantle closest to the core is hotter than the temperature closer to the crust.

Inner core

The inner core is located in the middle of the Earth. It is a ball of solid metals such as nickel and iron. The inner core is under pressure because of all the weight pushing on it from above. This pressure keeps the inner core in a solid state.

Crust

The thin outer layer of Earth is called the crust. The crust is made up of massive, irregularly shaped slabs of rock. These slabs are called tectonic plates.

Outer core

The outer core is located around the inner core. The outer core is made of iron and nickel. It is so hot that the metals are melted into liquid.

Tectonic plates

Earth's crust is broken into seven major tectonic plates, and many smaller ones. Tectonic plates are huge slabs of rock. The largest plates are named after the continents and oceans that sit on them. Plates beneath the oceans, called oceanic plates, are thinner and younger compared to continental plates. Continental plates are located under continents, and are much older and thicker. Plates are constantly moving. Scientists call this movement "creep." At the areas where plates meet, four things can happen:

One plate slides beneath another and forms a volcano and causes earthquakes.

The plates crash into one another, and scrunch up to form mountains.

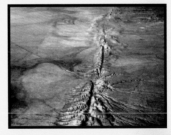

The plates slide roughly past one another, triggering earthquakes.

The plates move apart, in a process called sea-floor separating.

Plate Boundaries

The places where plates meet are called boundaries. At some boundaries, plates move easily past one another. At other boundaries, plates collide and scrunch up to form mountains or volcanoes. Some plates are even moving away from one another. Most earthquakes happen at the boundaries between plates.

Divergent boundaries

At divergent boundaries, plates move away from one another. As the plates separate, magma, or melted rock, rises from the mantle, filling the gap between the separating plates. The magma hardens, creating new crust on the edges of the two plates. Under the oceans, this process of separating plates and making new crust is called sea-floor spreading. When two continental plates diverge, or move apart, a rift valley is created, such as the Great Rift Valley in East Africa. Earthquakes at divergent boundaries are usually not very deep in the Earth's crust, and not very powerful.

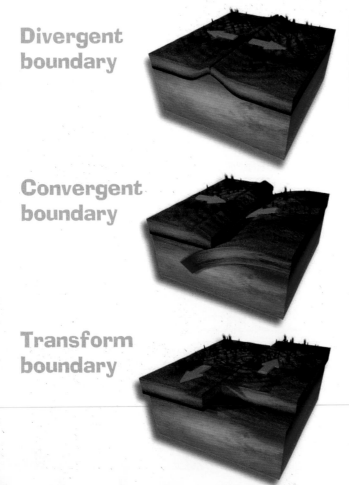

Divergent boundary

Convergent boundary

Transform boundary

About 35 million years ago, the African and Eurasian plates began to split, creating the Great Rift Valley in Africa. Today, these two continental plates are still separating.

(right) The Himalayan Mountains in Asia began to form 50 million years ago when two plates collided at a convergent boundary. The collision made one plate crumple up and slide over the other.

Convergent boundaries

At convergent boundaries, plates move toward each other. When they meet, one plate can slide below another in a process called subduction. Subduction usually happens where ocean plates slide under continental plates. Subduction created the Andes Mountains at the boundary of the Nazca Plate and the South American Plate, on the Pacific edge of South America. When two continental plates converge, the plates scrunch up to form mountains, such as the Himalaya Mountain range. Earthquakes at convergent boundaries begin deep in the crust and are strong and destructive.

Transform boundaries

At transform boundaries, two plates slide beside each other. Tectonic plates are huge, irregular shaped rocks with jagged edges. In some places, the plates stick as they try to pass. Pressure builds and when it becomes too great, the rocks crack, and an earthquake occurs. Most transform boundaries are on the ocean floor. One of the few transform boundaries on the surface is the San Andreas Fault in California.

The San Andreas Fault in California is part of the boundary between the North American Plate and the Pacific Plate.

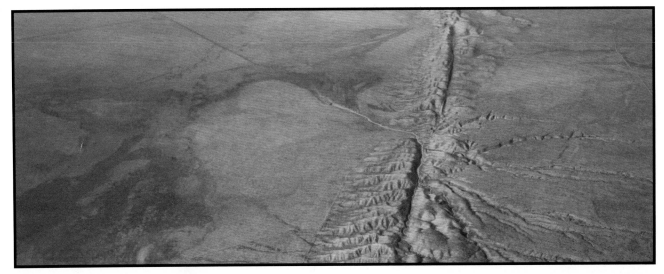

Faults

This fault is in Grotagja, Iceland.

Faults are fractures, or cracks, in the Earth's crust. These fractures happen at plate boundaries when the pressure becomes too great and results in an earthquake. Earthquakes most commonly occur at faults.

Some faults, called surface faults, can be seen from the ground, such as the San Andreas Fault in California. Others, called blind faults, lie beneath the surface. During an earthquake, one side of a fault suddenly slips. Faults are divided into **categories** depending on the way they slip. There are two main categories of faults: strike-slip faults and dip-slip faults.

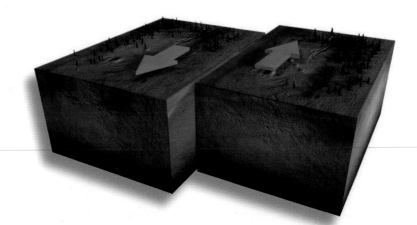

Strike-slip faults

Strike-slip faults are cracks where two pieces of rock move sideways and slide past each other. Transform faults are a type of strike-slip fault and happen at transform plate boundaries.

Dip-slip faults

The plates at dip-slip faults move up or down during an earthquake.
There are two types of dip-slip faults: normal and reverse faults.

In a normal fault, plates are pulled apart and one side moves down. Normal faults usually occur at divergent plate boundaries.

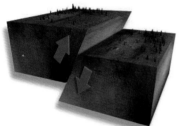

In a reverse fault, the plates are pushed together and one side moves up. Reverse faults happen at convergent plate boundaries.

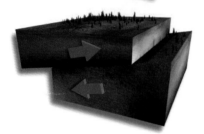

A thrust fault is a type of reverse fault. One rock moves up and over another. These faults usually occur where plates are being subducted.

Ring of Fire
The Ring of Fire is an area of subduction zones around the Pacific Ocean. A subduction zone occurs where an oceanic plate is pushed under another plate. About 80 per cent of major earthquakes happen along the Ring of Fire. The Ring of Fire also has more than half the world's active volcanoes.

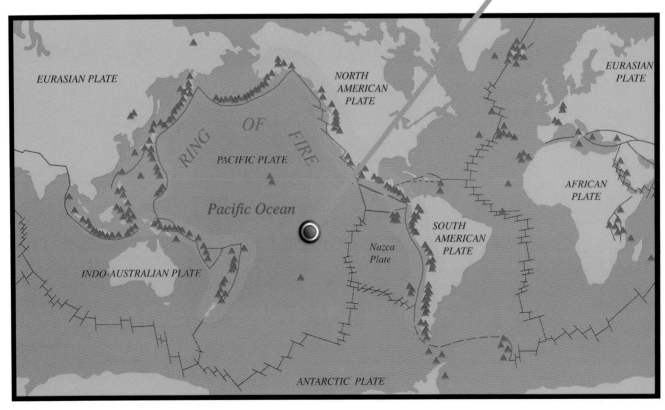

EURASIAN PLATE

NORTH AMERICAN PLATE

EURASIAN PLATE

RING OF FIRE

PACIFIC PLATE

AFRICAN PLATE

Pacific Ocean

SOUTH AMERICAN PLATE

Nazca Plate

INDO-AUSTRALIAN PLATE

ANTARCTIC PLATE

Seismic Waves

The spot underground where an earthquake occurs is called the focus, or hypocenter. The spot on the surface of the Earth above the focus is called the epicenter. The strongest shaking is usually felt near the epicenter of an earthquake.

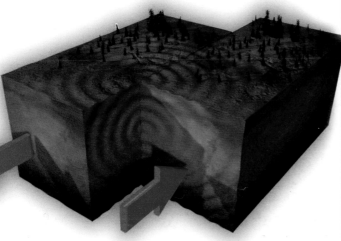

When a fault breaks, it changes the surface of the Earth. This change in the Earth's surface is **visible** and is called a static shift. A static shift can be seen where a road, railroad, or fence line built along the fault before the earthquake is twisted or bent after the quake. When the fault breaks it sends out waves of **energy** called seismic waves. Seismic waves are the **vibrations** we feel during an earthquake.

The shift in this agricultural field was formed by shifting fault lines during an earthquake in California, USA.

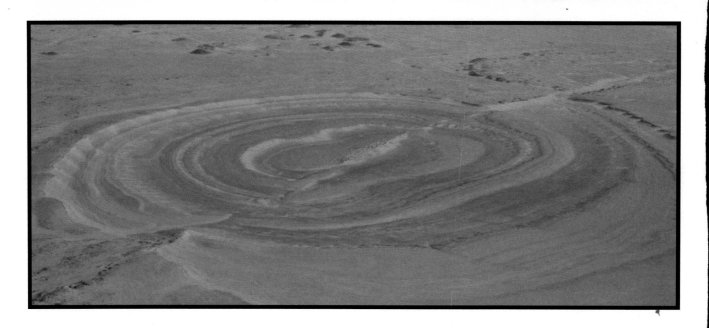

Doing the wave

There are two basic kinds of seismic waves: body waves and surface waves. Body waves travel outward in all directions, including down, from the focus of the earthquake. Surface waves only affect the Earth's surface, where they travel at slower speeds than body waves.

Seismic waves from this desert epicenter shaped the sand into a spiral pattern.

Shocking developments

An earthquake is usually a group of seismic waves. Foreshocks are smaller **tremors** that come before a large earthquake. Sometimes, these tremors are felt as a slight vibration and shaking. A large earthquake is called a mainshock. Aftershocks are tremors that follow. Aftershocks can happen weeks, months, or even years after a large earthquake. Usually, the larger the mainshock, the larger, longer, and more numerous the aftershocks there will be.

These rescue workers are carefully digging for survivors after a mainshock.

BODY WAVES

Body waves are the first type of seismic waves released during an earthquake. Body waves have little effect on Earth's surface. There are two types: P-Waves and S-Waves.

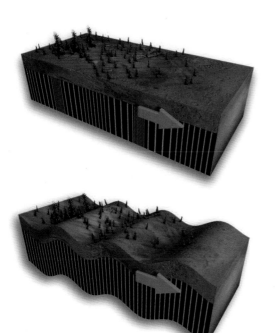

P-waves

P-waves, or **compression** waves, travel four miles (six kilometers) per second in the Earth's crust. P-waves move through solid rock, air, and fluids, such as water or the molten layers of the Earth. Usually, these waves are felt as a small bump. P-waves squeeze and stretch rock as they travel through it.

S-waves

S-waves move rock up and down as they travel through the Earth's crust. S-waves travel slower than P-waves, at about two miles (three kilometers) per second. S-waves can not travel through liquids or **gases**, so they do not pass through Earth's inner layers of molten rock and liquid metal.

SURFACE WAVES

There are two types of surface waves: Love waves and Rayleigh waves. Surface waves cause the most damage during an earthquake, even when they are far from the epicenter.

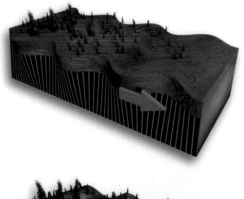

Love waves

Love waves are surface waves that travel through Earth's surface **horizontally** and move the ground from side to side. Love waves usually travel at about two miles (three kilometers) per second.

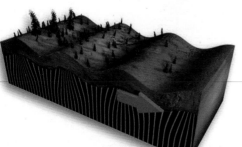

Rayleigh waves

Rayleigh waves make the surface of Earth roll like waves on the ocean. Rayleigh waves are the slowest of the seismic waves. They move at about two miles (three kilometers) per second.

(right) The crack in this salt flat in the western state of Gujarat, India, is over the epicenter of an earthquake. The waves that spread from the epicenter moved the salt in wave-like patterns. A salt flat is a lake that dried up, leaving a hard, crusty layer of salt on the surface.

Dhori village, India, 2001

Surface waves caused this highway to collapse in Santiago, Chile, almost 200 miles (317 km) from the epicenter.

Santiago, Chile, 2010

Working with Waves

Really powerful earthquakes are not everyday events, but when they do happen, earthquakes threaten lives and destroy property. Scientists cannot accurately predict the exact date and location of earthquakes. Seismologists are scientists who study seismic activity in the Earth. They use this information to monitor areas that have many earthquakes in order to estimate when one might occur.

Creep is the slow and steady movement along faults caused by moving plates. Seismologists use tools to keep track of creep, but they cannot distinguish between creep and foreshock until after an earthquake.

Measuring foreshocks

Seismologists use **laser beams** to track changes in fault lines. They beam light across a fault and can tell by the way the light reflects back whether the ground has moved. The laser beams record very small movements.

Seismologists use laser beams to detect small ground movements. This seismology station is near Parkfield, California, where movement along a fault is tracked.

Tools of the trade

A tiltmeter is an earthquake monitoring tool. It is a simple device of two water-filled pans joined by a pipe. When placed across a fault, with one pan on either side of the break, a tiltmeter detects movement in the Earth's crust when the water level in the pan increases or decreases. By measuring the water movement, seismologists can tell how much the Earth has moved.

Tiltmeter

Richter Scale

In the 1930s, American seismologist Charles F. Richter measured the peaks and valleys on a seismogram to determine the strength, or magnitude, of an earthquake. From his findings, he developed the Richter Scale to rate earthquakes. For every increase of one number on the scale, the earthquake is ten times more powerful.

Magnitude earthquake effects

2.5 or less	Usually not felt, but can be recorded by seismograph.
2.6 to 5.4	Often felt, but only causes minor damage.
5.5 to 6.0	Slight damage to buildings and other structures.
6.1 to 6.9	May cause a lot of damage in very populated areas.
7.0 to 7.9	Major earthquake causing serious damage.
8.0 or greater	A great earthquake that totally destroys communities near the epicenter.

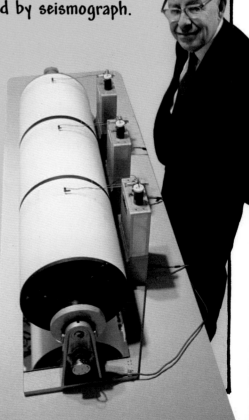

Charles Richter thought that buildings needed to be constructed better to survive earthquakes.

Measuring waves

A seismograph is an instrument used to measure seismic waves. It is made up of a heavy weight that hangs from a spring or wire. When the ground shakes, the weight appears to jiggle and bounce up and down or back and forth. Attached to the other end of the spring or wire is a pen that records the bumping of the weight onto a piece of paper. This is called a seismogram. When there is no movement in the ground, the pen draws a straight line. Powerful earthquakes have high peaks and low valleys on their seismograms.

Seismologists can now study seismograph readings on a computer screen.

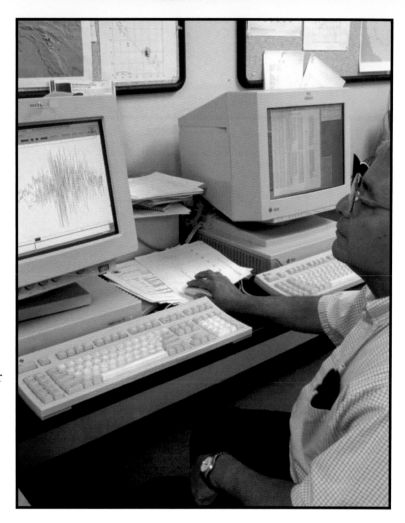

Ancient seismology

The first known instrument to record earthquakes dates back to around 100 A.D. in China. Geographer and astronomer Chang Heng invented the instrument to detect earthquakes too mild to be felt by humans. He wanted to determine what direction the quake's focus was. Heng's invention was a bronze vessel that had a hanging weight called a pendulum in the center. On the outside of the vessel was a ring of dragon heads holding bronze balls. Sitting around the vessel were toads with their mouths open. When the earth moved, the pendulum stayed still and the vessel moved. This caused a dragon's mouth to open and a ball to fall out.

Path of Destruction

Most of the damage an earthquake causes is not from the earthquake itself, but from its after-effects: tsunamis, liquefaction, landslides, mudslides, avalanches, and fires.

Tsunamis

Earthquakes beneath the ocean floor cause huge ocean waves called tsunamis. When the ocean floor moves up or down during an earthquake, a large amount of water is **displaced**, creating the wave. Tsunamis travel thousands of miles across the ocean at speeds of 597 miles per hour (960 km/h) or more. At sea, these waves are not very large, but as tsunamis near shorelines and shallower waters, the waves slow down and increase in height.

Aceh, Indonesia, 2004

(above) Following the 2004 earthquake in Indonesia, tsunamis devastated landmasses bordering the Indian Ocean with waves of up to 100 feet (30 meters) high.

Liquefaction

Liquefaction occurs in areas where the soil is loose or sandy. Strong quaking shakes the soil apart into individual grains. This causes the soil to loose strength and act as a liquid or wet quicksand. Buildings on the soil are no longer supported and topple. Once the shaking stops, the ground returns to its firm condition.

Japan, 2004

Soil liquefaction caused this sewer to float to the surface after an earthquake in Japan in 2004.

Indonesia, 2009

Landslides

A landslide is the rapid movement of soil, rocks, trees, and plants down a slope. The shaking of the surface generated by earthquakes loosens the soil and **debris** on the slope. Some landslides are slow-moving, while other landslides move so rapidly that they can destroy cities and kill people without warning.

Mudslides

Mudslides are fast-moving landslides that start on steep hillsides. As the mud forms, the slide can speed up to 35 miles per hour (56 km/h). Mudslides can be a watery mixture or thick, rocky debris. Mudslides are strong enough to wash away trees, cars, and homes.

Avalanches

An avalanche is a rapid slide of snow and ice down a mountainside or slope. They are often triggered by earthquakes. Avalanches can reach speeds of more than 200 miles per hour (322 km/h).

Rescue workers search the rubble for any signs of life in a village buried by a landslide. The landslide was triggered by an earthquake in West Sumatra, Indonesia. This village was just one of several that were destroyed by landslides from the earthquake.

Fire

During an earthquake, power lines may be knocked down and **natural gas** lines sometimes crack, causing fires. Often, water lines are also damaged during the earthquake. Without water to put out the fires, cities can burn to the ground.

San Francisco, California 1906

In the 1906 San Francisco earthquake, more than 90 per cent of the damage to buildings was caused by fire. The earthquake also caused a 290 mile (470 kilometer) crack in California's San Andreas Fault.

Port Royal, Jamaica

On June 7, 1692 a severe earthquake shook Port Royal, Jamaica. The sandy soil of Port Royal turned to quicksand because of liquefaction. The town residents and all their possessions sank into the earth. Once the earthquake stopped, the sand began to dry out and the people buried in the sand were squeezed to death, or were drowned by the tsunami that followed the quake. A lucky few who were swallowed by the sand were spit out by the ocean and rescued at sea.

The Big Ones

Most major earthquakes occur in areas where plates meet, such as California, Iran, and Japan. When the center of a plate is cracked, or has faults, earthquakes will occasionally happen there as well.

Indonesia

On December 26, 2004, Indonesia was hit with one of the deadliest natural disasters in history. An earthquake measuring between 9.1 and 9.3 on the Richter scale occurred off the west coast of Sumatra. It is the third largest earthquake ever recorded on a seismograph. Tsunamis generated by the earthquake traveled along the coast of the Indian Ocean, destroying land and structures, and killing more than 230,000 people. More than seven billion U.S. dollars in humanitarian aid was raised worldwide to help the countries affected by the disaster recover.

(below) The Aceh province in Indonesia was the closest land to the epicenter of the earthquake and therefore suffered the most damage.

Aceh, Indonesia, 2004

Chile

The largest recorded earthquake occurred in Chile on May 22, 1960. It measured 9.5 on the Richter scale. Aftershocks followed for days and severely damaged the southern part of the South American country. The earthquake left two million people homeless and caused tsunamis, killer landslides, and a volcanic eruption. The tsunamis drowned and injured people as far away as Hawaii and Japan. Landslides killed people in rural Chile. The Puyehue volcano in central Chile erupted two days after the mainshock. The shoreline in much of Chile changed forever after the earth thrusted up and down near the fault line. Another powerful earthquake hit Chile on February 10, 2010, reaching a magnitude of 8.8 and killing 486 people.

Valdivia, Chile, 1960

Quake aid

During an earthquake, people can be trapped under the rubble of buildings. Earthquake rescue teams must work quickly and carefully to extract people from the rubble. Humans can live a long time without food, but only days without water. Most successful extractions occur within hours or days of a quake. A number of disaster relief agencies, such as the Red Cross and the Red Crescent, work in earthquake zones as soon as an earthquake hits. Many countries depend on these relief agencies to help rescue people, provide hospital supplies, and infrastructure, such as roads, railways, communications, power, and water supply.

(top) Many buildings were destroyed by the earthquake in Chile in 1960.

(right) The Red Cross supplied thousands of people in Haiti with water immediately after the earthquake in 2010.

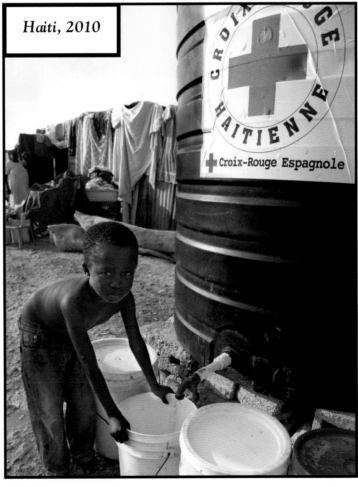

Haiti, 2010

Staying Safe

Most injuries from earthquakes are from falling objects and crumbling buildings and not from the actual movement of the ground. Dangers in the home include flying glass, falling bookcases, moving furniture, and fires.

(above) An earthquake in California caused merchandise in this store to fall off the shelves.

Earthquake drills

In parts of the world where earthquakes are common, such as Japan and California, children in school are taught to drop, cover, and hold. They drop under a desk or sturdy table and stay away from windows, bookcases, file cabinets, and other objects that could fall. Then they stay under cover until the shaking stops and hold onto the desk or table. If the desk or table moves, they are taught to move with it.

Dangers around us

People who live in areas where earthquakes commonly occur need to earthquake-proof their homes. They do this by imagining what would happen if their houses started to shake and planning for it. They look for:

- Furniture and heavy appliances that could tip
- Glass and other breakable objects on tables and in cabinets
- Flammable liquids such as painting and cleaning products stored close to sources of heat

Helpful hints

By planning and practicing what to do before an earthquake occurs, people can learn to react quickly when the shaking begins. Here are some guidelines for staying safe:

- Stay calm. If you are inside, stay inside. Go to a safe spot in a doorway, under a desk, or on the inside corner of the house. Stay away from windows or glass doors
- If on the road, drive away from bridges, stop in a safe area, and stay in the vehicle

Items to keep handy

It is a good idea to have some items on hand in case the power goes out. When severe earthquakes hit, an area is often left without electricity, running water, and heat for a couple of hours or even days.

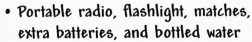

- Portable radio, flashlight, matches, extra batteries, and bottled water
- Manual can opener to open canned and dried foods. There should be enough food for a week for each person
- Portable stove, such as butane or charcoal, that can be used after making sure there is no possible gas leak in the area
- First Aid Kit including special medicines needed for family members

FIRST AID KIT
PREMIERS SOINS

What Science Can Do

To make structures that can withstand earthquakes, people who design and build buildings need to understand the stresses caused by the shaking. Scientists place instruments on buildings, bridges, and on the ground to measure how the structures react during an earthquake. Information is collected each time an earthquake hits. This information is used to improve and update building designs.

Built to last

Building codes are rules that builders must follow. In earthquake-prone areas, these codes are developed by studying buildings that crumbled during earthquakes. Buildings constructed to these codes are less likely to crumble and fall apart during an earthquake.

Today, earthquake monitoring instruments are installed in hospitals, bridges, and dams in earthquake-prone areas of the world. From these instrument readings, scientists have learned what building methods and materials can endure an earthquake. Improvements to older buildings are made so they too can withstand an earthquake's destructive forces.

Along with changing how buildings are constructed, where they are built is also very important. Solid rock and stable soil are the best locations. Even the best designed buildings will not survive if they are built on ground that could liquefy during an earthquake.

(right) The Transamerica building in downtown San Francisco, California, was specially designed to survive an earthquake.

A researcher in California studies the effects of earthquakes on buildings by shaking a model of a house, then assessing the damage.

Making it safe

One way to earthquake-proof is to **reinforce** the bottom of the building to the upper part of the building with metal **cables**. That way, when the ground shakes, the two pieces move as a unit, instead of having the upper floors topple. Another way is to design the upper part of the building to move separately from the bottom, so that even if the ground shakes, the building will remain in one place.

Bridges

Intact bridges and roadways are important for an area to recover quickly from an earthquake. They are necessary to deliver rescuers, medical supplies, food, and water. In earthquake-prone areas, many bridges have reinforced columns that help ensure the bridge does not collapse.

This expressway tipped onto its side after a 7.2 magnitude earthquake hit in Kobe, Japan.

Kobe, Japan 1995

How Nature Knows

Some animals have much better hearing than humans and may be able to sense foreshocks that are too weak for humans to feel.

Animal signs

There have been many reports of animals' strange behavior before an earthquake. Catfish are said to become restless before earthquakes, and at times have been reported to leap out of water onto dry land. Mice appear dazed before earthquakes and can easily be caught. Snakes have been found frozen on the snow, because they have left their winter hibernation before an earthquake. Hens have been reported laying fewer eggs, or no eggs at all before earthquakes. Bees have been seen leaving their hive in a rush, minutes before an earthquake, and then not returning until fifteen minutes after the earthquake ends.

There are other signs in nature that warn us of an earthquake. Ponds and lakes may become muddy, and gas bubbles appear at the surface of the water. Scientists say that these phenomena may be caused by gases escaping from the earth as rocks shift.

While it is now generally accepted by scientists that animals do sometimes behave oddly before an earthquake, these behaviors are not dependable enough to be used to predict earthquakes.

Watching for animal behavior helped researchers in China predict an earthquake in 1974.

These "earthquake detectors" are from Mexico. When ground movement occurs, the animals' heads and tails shake.

China's early warning

In the 1970s, people in China were taught to watch signs in nature to try and predict earthquakes. The Chinese government built 250 seismograph stations, and trained 100,000 people to measure movements in the Earth because of the many earthquakes there.

On February 4, 1974, people reported signs of a possible earthquake in Liaoning Province in northeast China. People were told to leave their homes and the area was evacuated. Later the same day, a 7.3 magnitude earthquake hit. Almost all buildings in the town were damaged or destroyed by the earthquake, but very few people were harmed.

Unfortunately, the same signs did not appear before the devastating earthquake in Tangshan, northern China, in July 1976. It was a powerful 7.8 earthquake, which resulted in 750,000 deaths. China now relies less on animal behavior as a prediction of earthquakes, but researchers are still watching nature's warning signs.

Recipe for Disaster

Try this earthquake experiment to understand plate tectonics and convection currents.

What you need:
* Foam pieces shaped like the continents that fit loosely together
* A large heat-resistant pan, such as a metal cooking pot
* Water
* A direct heat source, such as a stove or burner
* Food coloring
* Adult supervision

What to do:

1. Place the cooking pot filled with water on a stove or hot plate without turning on the heat. Arrange foam continents close together forming a large continent.

2. Turn the heat on, directly below the floating continents. Do not allow water to boil. Watch as the continents drift apart as the water begins to warm up. They are moving because of convection currents in the water.

3. Remove the continents and let the water settle. While the pan is still over the heat, place a few drops of food coloring in the water. Watch closely and allow it to naturally flow with the convection current.

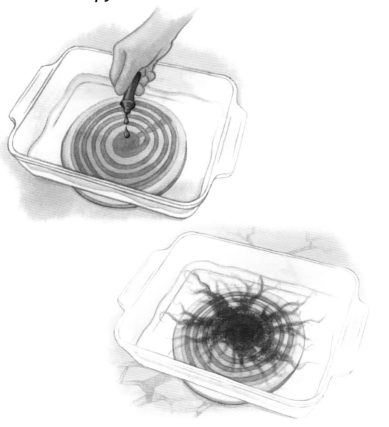

4. Draw a picture showing how the food coloring moved in a circular motion.

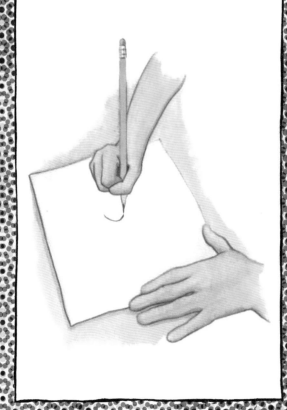

What you will see:

The foam pieces move because of friction between the water and foam. The water rises and separates and these form the convection currents. Think about how powerful convection in the mantle must be in order to move huge tectonic plates. There must be a lot of heat down there!

200 million years ago

Today

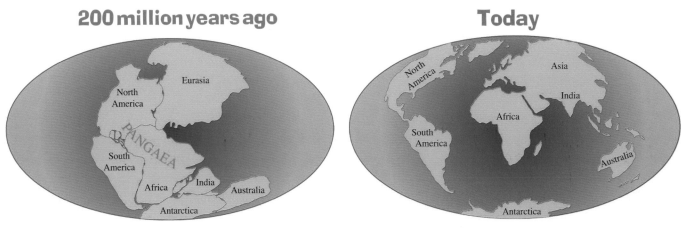

Scientists believe that at one time all the continents were joined together in a giant land mass called Pangaea. Over time, the continents drifted apart to their present state, and are still moving today.

31

Glossary

astronomer A scientist who studies the stars and planets

cables A strong, thick rope made of strands of steel wire

categories Divisions or groupings within a system

compression Squeezed or pressed tightly together

debris Scattered fragments of something that has been destroyed

displaced Put out of the usual place

energy Power for doing work

flammable Able to easily catch fire

gas A substance that is neither liquid or solid

horizontally Describing something that is level or straight across

laser beams Powerful rays of light

natural gas A colorless gas burned for cooking and heating homes

predict To tell about in advance

pressure Weight pushing on an object

reinforce To make stronger with more support

seismic activity Earthquakes and movements of Earth's crust

stresses Physical pressure or strain

tremors The shaking movement of the earth

vibrations Rapid back-and-forth movements

visible Able to be seen

Index

Websites

This site from National Geographic features a simulation of different forces of nature and the damage they do under various conditions.
http://environment.nationalgeographic.com/environment/natural-disasters/forces-of-nature.html?section=t

Get all your earthquake questions answered at:
www.weatherwizkids.com/weather-earthquake.htm